SOCCER'S Greatest Clubs

Juventus FC

Kevin Snow

Cavendish Square
New York

Published in 2021 by Cavendish Square Publishing, LLC
243 5th Avenue, Suite 136, New York, NY 10016

First Edition

Website: cavendishsq.com

Library of Congress Cataloging-in-Publication Data

Names: Snow, Kevin, author.
Title: Juventus FC / Kevin Snow.
Description: New York : Cavendish Square, 2021. | Series: Soccer's greatest clubs | Includes bibliographical references and index.
Identifiers: LCCN 2019020897 (print) | LCCN 2019021842 (ebook) | ISBN 9781502652713 (library bound) | ISBN 9781502652706 (pbk) | ISBN 9781502652720 (ebook)
Subjects: LCSH: Juventus (Soccer club)--History--Juvenile literature. | Soccer teams--Italy--Turin--Juvenile literature.
Classification: LCC GV943.6.J88 S66 2021 (print) | LCC GV943.6.J88 (ebook) | DDC 796.334/64094512--dc23
LC record available at https://lccn.loc.gov/2019020897
LC ebook record available at https://lccn.loc.gov/2019021842

Editor: Kristen Susienka
Copy Editor: Rebecca Rohan
Designer: Joe Parenteau

The photographs in this book are used by permission and through the courtesy of: Cover, pp. 11 (bottom), 53 cristiano barni/Shutterstock.com; series art (badge) Onur Cem/Shutterstock.com; series art (field) comzeal images/Shutterstock.com; series art (soccer ball) FocusStocker/Shutterstock.com; series art (crowd silhouette) Nosyrevy/Shutterstock.com; p. 4 GIUSEPPE CACACE/AFP/Getty Images; p. 9 AP Photo; pp. 10, 14, 23 courtesy of Wikimedia Images; p. 11 (top) Central Press/Hulton Archive/Getty Images; p. 12 The Picture Art Collection/Alamy Stock Photo; p. 15 News Press/Getty Images; p. 18 Bob Thomas/Getty Images; p. 19 Marco Canoniero/Light Rocket via Getty Images; p. 21 History and Art Collection/Alamy Stock Photo; p. 26 Pier Marco Tacca/Anadolu Agency/Getty Images; p. 28 Tony Marshall/EMPICS via Getty Images; p. 30 Giuseppe Bellini/Getty Images; p. 32 ninopavisic/Shutterstock.com; p. 34 Juventus FC/Juventus FC via Getty Images; p. 35 Matteo Bottanelli/NurPhoto via Getty Images; pp. 36, 39 Liverpool Echo/Mirrorpix/Getty Images; p. 43 malgosia janicka/Shutterstock.com; p. 45 Etsuo Hara/Getty Images; pp. 48, 51 Valerio Pennicino - Juventus FC/Juventus FC via Getty Images.

CPSIA compliance information: Batch #CS20CSQ: For further information contact Cavendish Square Publishing LLC, New York, New York, at 1-877-980-4450.

Printed in the United States of America

TABLE OF CONTENTS

Alessandro Del Piero is joined by his Juventus teammates to celebrate an important victory in 2012.

1 MEET JUVENTUS

Soccer is a sport that started centuries ago. It has been played by kings and peasants. Today, it's one of the most popular sports in the world. It has many good teams. Other places in the world call soccer "football," but in America "football" is a very different sport.

WHAT IS SOCCER?

Soccer is played by two teams. Each team tries to get one ball in the other team's net. They work together to move the ball down the playing field, or pitch. Soccer players can't use their hands to guide the ball forward. They can use their feet, chest, and head, though.

A TOP TEAM

One of the top soccer teams in Europe today is an Italian team called Juventus (yoo-VEN-tuss) Football Club (FC). It's a true definition of a dynasty, or a long-ruling group. To be thought of as a dynasty in professional sports is a great accomplishment for a team. Not only does it mean the team has had success, but it also means the team has been successful for a number of years. With that success also comes championships—in many cases, championships won several years in a row, not just once in a while. Winning many championships is usually the sign of a very talented team.

Juventus began in 1897. It had successes and failures in its first few decades, but eventually it became an excellent team. It joined Italy's Serie A league when the league was formed in 1929. Serie A is the top level of Italian professional soccer. Today, many people think Serie A is one of the best leagues in the world. From 1931 to 1935, Juventus won five Serie A titles in a row.

Before Serie A started, teams in Italy would play for the Italian Football Championship each year. The first year of this league was 1898 and only included four teams. Juventus's first season in this Italian league was 1900.

As soccer's popularity grew, more teams were added throughout Italy over the years. These teams would play in groups located in different parts of the country. Soon, there was a need for a new league.

SPORT SHORT

In addition to being Juventus's hometown, Turin, located in northern Italy, is also the chocolate capital of Europe. It has a 10-day chocolate festival every spring.

WHAT DOES IT MEAN?

Juventus started in 1897 when a group of high school students in Turin decided to form the Sport-Club Juventus. Juventus *is the Latin word for "youth." The team switched its name to Foot-Ball Club Juventus in 1900. Now, the team is also known as Juventus, Juve (YOO-vey), or* I Bianconera *(which means "the black and whites"—because of their jerseys).*

Serie A was created to be the top league in Italy. For the first season, 1929–1930, there were 18 teams in Serie A, including Juventus.

Today, Juventus continues to be a top team in Italy. Maintaining a top level of play hasn't been easy, though. Many talented players have helped the team become what it is today. In Turin, the city where Juventus plays, the club's success has taken hard work and a special club mission that started in 1923.

That year, the team was bought by the Agnelli family. The Agnellis helped the team develop itself around an idea of unity. Today, the club's rule is that no one player is bigger than the group. No matter how talented or famous a player is, putting on a Juventus jersey means the person will work hard to make the team proud.

The Agnelli family helped make Juventus a successful, determined team. Before long, the team was drawing many good players from other parts of Europe and forming a powerful club. Today, Juventus continues to have many international players wearing their jersey.

SUCCESS AT HOME AND AWAY

In the 21st century, the club has had wins at home and around the world. As of 2019, they've won 13 championships in the Coppa Italia competition, including 4 straight wins from 2015 to 2018. Coppa Italia is a tournament that happens once a year. It features teams from all four levels of the Italian professional leagues. With Serie A being the highest level, the top eight teams from Serie A are automatically allowed into the round before the quarterfinal.

Juventus has won the Union of European Football Association (UEFA) Cup three times and two UEFA Champions League titles as of 2019. UEFA is the governing body of European soccer. The Champions League is one of the most famous events on the soccer calendar. Many top teams from across Europe compete in it. Juventus's first Champions League title came in 1985 against Liverpool when the event was known as the Champions Cup. It was renamed the Champions League in 1992.

In addition to their on-field titles, Juventus was twice—in 1993 and 1996—recognized as the top soccer team in the world by the International Federation of Football History and Statistics (IFFHS). In 2000, they

Juventus won its first European Champion's Cup in 1985 over Liverpool. This event is now known as the Champion's League.

were seventh overall in FIFA's ranking of the Top Clubs of the Century. FIFA was founded in France and stands for Fédération Internationale de Football Association, or the International Federation of Association Football in English. FIFA is a group that helps to plan important tournaments and soccer leagues all over the world.

STAR POWER

Juventus's stars have come from many different places. Forward John Charles was a top player in England before he joined the team in 1957. Charles became an instant hit with fans when he led the team to a Serie A title in his first year while also leading the league with 28 goals.

From left to right: Omar Sivori, John Charles, and Giampiero Boniperti pose together.

Much of Charles's success was due to the great teamwork he developed with forwards Giampiero Boniperti and Omar Sivori. They were even called "the Magical Trio" because they worked so well together. Boniperti played his entire career with Juventus and was team president from 1971 to 1990.

Juventus struck gold again in 1982 when they signed Michel Platini from France. Considered one of soccer's rising stars, Platini joined a Juventus team that included Italian superstar Paolo Rossi. That year, Rossi won the Ballon d'Or trophy, which is given to Europe's player of the year.

Platini and Rossi helped Juventus win many Serie A titles and European victories. Platini also received the Ballon d'Or in 1983, 1984, and 1985.

The team has also had two of the best goalkeepers to ever play the game, Gianluigi Buffon and Dino Zoff. Both men excelled in Serie A and European competition and represented Italy in many World Cups.

The list of iconic players who have contributed to the club's success over the years is endless. Modern Juventus teams have also featured some of Italy's

Goalkeeper Dino Zoff (*far right*) led Juventus to six Serie A titles in 11 seasons. Zoff also starred with the Italian national team.

best players, like Sebastian Giovinco, Andrea Pirlo, Leonardo Bonucci, and Arturo Vidal. Known as "La Pirana," a nickname referring to the carnivorous piranha fish whose aggression he seemed to mimic on the field, Vidal played with Juventus from 2011 to 2015.

The club's reputation has made it popular with many people in Italy and around the world. With its sense of confidence, belief in teamwork, and excellent players, it will continue to have success in years to come.

Miralem Pjanic from Bosnia joined Juventus in 2016.

A Juventus team from the early 1900s is shown here.

2

A HISTORY IN ITALY

Many dreams have been born on park benches over the years. As the story goes, that's exactly how Juventus FC came to life. It was November 1897, and some teenagers from Turin, Italy, met together to share their love of soccer. The students decided to form a sports club. They called it Sport-Club Juventus. Two years later, the group was renamed Foot-Ball Club Juventus. Now, the team is simply known as Juventus FC. Its history is long and full of ups and downs—and different-colored uniforms.

THE BLACK AND WHITE

In its early days, the team played games wearing pink shirts and black ties. As the pink tops began to fade over time, the players needed new uniforms. John Savage was an Englishman on the Juventus staff. His job was to help find the team new uniforms. Savage reached out to a friend back home for some advice. His friend connected him with a team called the Notts County Magpies in Nottingham, England, one of the oldest soccer clubs in the world.

The early Juventus game uniforms featured pink shirts. They switched to the iconic black and white in 1903.

The Magpies wore uniforms with black and white stripes on them. Savage made a deal to have the Magpies' old jerseys shipped to Turin for Juventus. Soon after, history was made. The iconic black-and-white-striped look has been part of Juventus since 1903. The color scheme is also why the team's Italian nickname is I Bianconera, or "the black and whites."

Two years after adopting the black and white colors, Juventus captured its first Italian "scudetto," or "little shield" badge, by winning the 1905 Prima Categoria, or first division, season title. Scudetto badges are worn by the team that wins the league championship each season. Since Juventus won the league Prima Categoria, they got to put that badge on their jerseys.

During the 1905 season, Juventus played in a league with Genoa and US Milanese. They played two games

JUVENTUS/TORINO: A RIVALRY

Juventus's Cristiano Zanetti (*right*) collides with a Torino defender (*left*) in 2007.

Known as the Derby della Mole, Juventus and Torino have the oldest continuing derby between two teams based in the same city. The derby's name comes from Mole Antonelliana, a famous building in the city of Turin. It's believed to be the tallest museum in the world. In Italian, mole is defined as a building of great proportions.

"Great" would also describe the passion displayed in these games, first played in 1907. Much of this comes from the early days of each team. As the Agnelli ownership developed later, Juventus has played the role of a wealthy, powerful team, and Torino represented the region's working class.

While both clubs have taken turns winning these games, over a 20-year span Juventus never lost a match to Torino. From April 1995 to April 2015, Juventus posted 13 wins and 4 ties against their rivals. On April 26, 2015, that streak was broken when Torino won 2–1. The rivalry is one that will most likely continue as long as the two teams exist.

SPORT SHORT

The black and white colors used by Juventus are considered to be aggressive and powerful.

against each team, finishing first overall with a record of two wins and two ties.

Before Serie A began in 1929, the Italian professional league had teams located in different parts of the country. Teams were grouped together by their location, not by skill level. There were normally three or four teams in each group. The first-place team from each group would then take part in a playoff tournament with the winners from the other groups. The team that collected the most points was declared the winner of the Prima Categoria as the best team in Italy.

The version of Serie A that we know now was started in the 1929–1930 season. The teams were grouped together in one league for the entire country. There were 18 teams in the first season. That format was kept until 2004, when changes increased the amount of teams to 20.

The Serie A season runs from August to May. There are 38 games in the season. The schedule has each team play each other twice, once at home and once away, or at a different stadium. The season is divided into two 19-game segments. The first half of the season is called the *andata* (going), and the second half is called the *ritorno* (return). Teams play each opponent once per segment, and the order of how the teams play each other stays the same each segment. The only thing that changes for each segment is where the game is played.

Teams receive three points for a win, one for a tie (draw), and zero for a loss. The first-place team each season receives the scudetto as league champion. In addition, the champion and runner-up team receive an automatic spot in the UEFA Champions League playoffs. The third-place team is awarded an opportunity to qualify for the Champions League playoffs.

The teams that finish in the last three spots in the league are relegated (dropped) to Serie B, the second level in Italian professional soccer, for the next season. They are replaced in Serie A by the top three teams in Serie B, who are promoted (moved up) for the following season.

LOOKING FOR STRUCTURE

The early years of Juventus were a tough time in the team's history. Team president Alfred Dick led the team to the 1905 league championship, but the team's board of directors didn't like his rough business style. The board of directors are the group of people that supervise how a team or company is run.

Following the 1906 season, Dick was fired by the board. He then took some players and staff members with him to create Torino FC. This meant that the city of Turin now had two professional soccer teams. This unique situation created the annual Derby della Mole, which is still played today between Juventus and Torino. A derby is a game played between two teams in the

GIOVANNI TRAPATTONI

Giovanni Trapattoni is shown here at a Juventus match in 1978.

After a successful playing career that included an appearance in the 1962 World Cup for Italy, Giovanni Trapattoni became one of the best managers in European soccer. Trapattoni coached Juventus from 1976 to 1986, and again from 1991 to 1994. It was during his first time with the club that he became part of team history.

Trapattoni's teams captured six Italian League championships and two Coppa Italias, and he became the first European soccer coach to capture all three European championships (European Cup, European Super Cup, and European Cup Winners' Cup) with one team.

Trapattoni is Juventus's all-time coaching leader in games coached (596), wins (319), and trophies earned (14). Trapattoni's coaching career ended in 2010, but it included coaching German team Bayern Munich and Portuguese team Benfica, along with both the Italian and Irish national teams. He finished his career as one of five coaches to win titles in four different countries.

same city or region. Derbies help create passion and a spirit of rivalry among the fans of both teams.

Juventus needed to have a good chairman if they wanted to win a lot. Chairmen help make business decisions, hire coaches, and bring players to the team. From 1907 to 1923, six different chairmen were elected by the board of directors to oversee team operations after Dick left.

Whether it's sports or business, a successful organization is built on structure that begins at the top. Creating stability is important to becoming successful. This is exactly what Juventus needed. By having 6 different people in charge of the team over 16 years, Juventus wasn't able to run their business properly. Then, Juventus met the Agnelli family.

THE RISE OF THE AGNELLIS

The ideal team owner has a vision for the future and a passion for winning. Modern teams like the New York Yankees of Major League Baseball are an example of a team that has succeeded because of strong ownership. The late George Steinbrenner built them into one of the best teams in baseball and one of the most popular and most recognizable sports teams in the world.

Team president Andrea Agnelli inspects the field prior to a 2019 Champions League game.

The same credit can be given to the Agnelli family, who bought Juventus in 1923. Now celebrating almost 100 years of ownership, the

Agnellis' majority leadership of Juventus is the longest lasting of any professional sports team in the world.

BUYING THE CLUB

Giovanni Agnelli was the first Agnelli owner of Juventus. He became an excellent businessman in Italy after he started the FIAT motor company in 1899. FIAT is now a worldwide company and is still very popular. Agnelli had been a soccer fan for many years. He bought Juventus in 1923 for an unknown price.

After taking over the team, Giovanni Agnelli made his son, Edoardo, the team president. He would be the first of four Agnellis to oversee Juventus. As of 2019, Edoardo's grandson, Andrea, is Juventus's chairman of the board. He has been since 2010.

The team had brought in respected Hungarian coach Jenő Károly in 1923. Károly had been one of Hungary's best scorers during his playing days. He then moved on to coach Savona in the Italian league from 1920 to 1923 before coaching Juventus.

The Agnellis knew they needed some better players. They looked again to Hungary, this time adding striker Ferenc Hirzer for the 1925–1926 season. Hirzer had played the previous two years in Germany and the Czech Republic. He knew Károly's coaching style and decided to join Juventus. Hirzer scored three goals (also called a hat trick) in his first game against fellow Italian team Parma. He ended the year with a league-leading 35 goals.

Juventus won 19 games and finished in first place in 1925–1926. This was their first Italian league championship in 20 years. It was smart moves like signing Hirzer that would set the tone for years to come.

THE GOLDEN YEARS

While the first years of the Agnelli ownership helped set up the team for future success, it was in the 1930s that Juventus truly began to become a powerful Italian team. The 1929–1930 season was the first year of the Serie A league. Juventus finished third. They had a record of 19 wins, 8 losses, and 7 ties. It was a very successful start to their top-league career. Things were only going to get better.

In what's known in club history as "the golden five-year period," Juventus won five Serie A championships in a row, from 1930 to 1935. During this remarkable stretch, they won 115 of 166 games and lost just 21 times. To do this, Juventus relied on a number of homegrown Italian players. These players grew together to help the team win many games and championships.

The "golden five-year period" saw Juventus win five straight Serie A titles from 1930 to 1935. This team won the 1932–1933 scudetto.

The top players who helped were Giovanni Ferrari, Felice Borel, Gianpiero Combi, and Mario Varglien. One of the greatest Italian players of all time, forward Giovanni Ferrari was part of all five of Juventus's "golden" teams. Felice Borel scored 130 goals for Juventus and remains among the team's all-time leading scorers. Goalkeeper Gianpiero Combi played with Juventus from 1921 to 1934 and won four Serie A titles during his time there. Midfielder Mario Varglien was the captain of their first four Serie A championship teams and played with Juventus from 1927 to 1942.

What made these players even more appealing to fans throughout Italy was their presence on the national team when Italy won the World Cup in 1934. Juventus quickly became the favorite team of many soccer fans throughout the country.

REGIONAL STRUGGLES, GLOBAL APPEAL

Even though Juventus is popular in Italy, the team has not always been liked in its hometown. There was a time when it wasn't unusual to see more Juventus fans at away games than at home. Historically, fans from working-class Turin have supported Torino, while the rest of the country has cheered for Juventus. After the Agnellis bought Juventus, locals thought it was a team for the upper class, or wealthy. Many people in Turin didn't like that. They wanted a team that could represent them. That honor went to Torino, which people considered a team for the average worker.

People could really notice how few Turin fans the club had whenever Juventus played home games at the Stadio delle Alpi stadium from 1990 to 2006. The stadium was built to host the World Cup in 1990, and it could hold almost 70,000 fans. With the majority of Juventus fans based outside of Turin, the team would often play in front of thousands of empty seats. It's one of the reasons the team "downsized" to a total of 41,000 seats when they built Juventus Stadium in 2011.

COPPA SUCCESS

After their fifth straight Serie A title in 1935, Juventus would finish no higher than second place until 1943. They even dropped as low as eighth in the 1938–1939 season.

One highlight for Juventus was their first Coppa Italia victory in 1938. Coppa Italia is a tournament played each year between all four levels of Italian soccer. The first tournament was played in 1922, but it didn't become a yearly competition until 1935.

In 1938, Juventus advanced to the quarterfinals of the competition, where they defeated Atalanta 6–0. In

Juventus won the Coppa Italia for the first time in 1938. Coppa Italia is an annual tournament for all four levels of Italian soccer.

the semifinal they had another shutout in a 2–0 win over the powerful Ambrosiana-Inter. That set up a two-game final with their rivals from Torino. In soccer, each game of a playoff series against one team is referred to as a "leg." The winner is decided on aggregate score, which is the total score from both games. Juventus won the first leg 3–1, and the second leg 2–1. This meant they won the Coppa Italia championship with an aggregate score of 5–2. Juventus won their second Coppa Italia in 1942, when they defeated AC Milan.

RETURNING TO GLORY

During World War II, violence and warfare throughout the country canceled two seasons of professional soccer in Italy from 1943 to 1945. After the war, soccer was one of the things that helped the country recover. Juventus played a big part in that.

Giampiero Boniperti became an important player during this time. The 20-year-old Boniperti had spent three seasons with the Juventus youth team before playing his first Serie A game in March 1947. The Juventus youth program has been around for 70 years. This program allows kids to train and possibly play for Juventus when they get older. Many of the top players in team history came from the youth program.

During the 1947–1948 season, Boniperti was the top scorer in Serie A. Boniperti then teamed up with Danish forward John Hansen to lead Juventus to win Serie A titles in 1949–1950 and again in 1951–1952.

Juventus became the first team in Italy to win their 10th Serie A title in 1957–1958. This meant they could add a golden star to their jersey to signify winning

10 titles. The team has since earned the right to add 2 more stars with their 20th (1981–1982) and 30th (2013–2014) Serie A titles.

Juventus won just three Serie A titles in the 1960s. They did well again during the 1970s, with five Serie A titles in seven years from 1971 to 1978.

Leading the way was Italian superstar Roberto Bettega. He also started his career with the Juventus youth program at age 11. Bettega played 13 seasons with Juventus from 1969 to 1983 and won seven Serie A titles. He led the team in goal scoring five times. Bettega is the third all-time goal-scorer in Juventus history as of 2020, with 178 goals.

Juventus added four more Serie A titles in the 1980s. With star players like Michel Platini and Paolo Rossi, they also won major European competitions, including three European titles in one calendar year. This started with a win over Portuguese team Porto in May 1984 at the European Cup Winners' Cup. That was followed in January 1985 by a 2–0 win against English team Liverpool in the European Super Cup. Juventus then won the first European Cup title in team history with a 1–0 victory over Liverpool in May 1985. The team that had taken over Italy was now showing all of Europe they meant business.

Paulo Dybala celebrates a goal during a Serie A game against FC Crotone in 2017.

3 AWARDS, TITLES, AND SUCCESSES

The plan that the Agnelli family put in place nearly 100 years ago is still as evident in the 21st century as it was then. The players may change over the years, but the goal for the team is always the same: Put the team first. The titles and trophies won in the 1980s and 1990s have only driven the team to be even more successful with each new season.

With their 3–0 win over fellow Italian team Crotone on May 21, 2017, Juventus clinched its sixth consecutive Serie A scudetto. This also set an Italian league record. Following the game, a story on the team's official website detailed this historic accomplishment. However, it wasn't the usual game recap. Instead, it reminded fans of the club's overall vision. It read:

> *Anyone searching for the so-called secret to Juventus' success will [also] discover the most beautiful element not only of this illustrious club, but of sport. No individual is ever more important than the collective*

and few teams embody that better than this one has.

These words could've described any number of wins over the years. They were another reminder of the Juventus FC philosophy that started with the Agnelli purchase in 1923. That philosophy is still on display now, as the club remains one of the best soccer teams in European history.

EUROPEAN INVASION

Continued success in the Italian League has allowed Juventus to compete in some of the biggest UEFA tournaments throughout Europe. Individual teams can qualify for UEFA events based on their standing within their own leagues in the previous season. Juventus first played in a UEFA event in the 1959 European Cup. A few years later, they started winning. Beginning in

Gianluca Vialli (*left*) kicks a ball past two Ajax players during the 1996 UEFA Champions League final. Juventus won the game on penalty kicks.

1963 and continuing until 1991, they played in 28 UEFA events in a row—the most of any Italian club.

Juventus has also won twice in the Champions League competition. This is one of Europe's most popular yearly club contests. Juventus's wins happened in 1985 and 1996. They defeated English team Liverpool in 1985 and needed penalty kicks to beat Ajax from the Netherlands in 1996. They've also finished second seven times, including twice during the time when the contest was called the Champions Cup. In total, Juventus has won 11 international competitions as of 2020 and are the only team to have won each of the six UEFA events.

THE PERFECT SEASON

The 2011–2012 season featured several firsts for Juventus. It was the first season in their shiny new stadium, Juventus Stadium. It was also the first season for new manager Antonio Conte. Most importantly, that season, Juventus claimed their first Serie A title since 2002–2003. They also became the first team in league history to go undefeated in the 38-game format with a record of 23 wins and 15 ties. They scored 68 goals and only allowed 20 in the 38 games.

The only time the team struggled was a seven-game stretch where they had one win and six ties. They only scored three goals in these seven games. That was followed immediately by a season-high eight straight wins from March 17 to April 29. They outscored their opponents 23–1, with seven shutouts (games where their opponent didn't score) in the eight games.

This "dream season" for Juventus was also part of a 49-game Serie A undefeated streak that started

Mirko Vucinic (*left*) of Juventus uses his head against a ball in a game against Napoli in 2011.

on May 22, 2011, which was the final game of the 2010–2011 season. After going undefeated in 2011–2012, the 2012–2013 season for Juventus started with nine wins and one tie in their first ten games. Juventus finished with a total of 32 wins and 17 ties during the 49-game streak.

The historic 2011–2012 season also started another kind of winning streak. From then until 2019, Juventus won eight straight Serie A league titles. This included the club's 30th league title in 2013–2014. The 2019–2020 season also started with promising results, giving fans hope that another title was on the way.

WRITTEN IN THE STARS

Many soccer teams have a star on their jersey representing a major event in the team's history. The most common use of one star is to show the team has won 10 league titles. Juventus is one of the teams that does this. With their 30th league title victory in 2013–2014, Juventus players were able to add a third star to their jersey.

JUVENTUS DOING GOOD

Like many professional sports teams around the world, Juventus has used its popularity to give back to the community through charity. A statement on the Juventus.com website reads, "The club plays an active role in supporting a wide range of projects which are geared towards instilling the Juventus sporting values and ideals into society at large." Juventus has raised a lot of money for the Piedmont Foundation for Cancer Research and the Sant'Anna Hospital's new building to provide the highest levels of medical care possible for newborn children with illnesses. Its most well-known partnership has been with UNESCO's "Colour? What Colour?" project. The goal of the partnership is to help keep all racism and discrimination out of soccer. Juventus used social media platforms like Facebook and Instagram to help spread the message and bring awareness to fans, including giving tips on how they could stop racism throughout the entire soccer world.

At first, Juventus president Andrea Agnelli didn't want to add the third star. He was still upset about the team losing its Serie A titles in 2005 and 2006 because they were part of a scandal known as the Calciopoli scandal. "Calciopoli" means "football corruption." Juventus was one of four teams punished for their involvement in trying to use referees to help decide the outcomes of their games between 2004–2005 and 2005–2006. This type of behavior isn't allowed in professional sports.

Agnelli explained to ESPN.com on May 6, 2014: "We're not putting the third star on our shirts. For us, we have thirty-two scudettos, even if only thirty of them are being counted. Then when somebody else manages to be able to put a second star on their shirt, we will add the third to ours, just to emphasize the difference." Agnelli eventually changed his mind, however. The team added the third star when they introduced their new Adidas uniforms in 2015–2016.

Juventus has three stars on its jersey to celebrate winning 30 Italian League titles.

Juventus also won the Coppa Italia four straight years, from 2014 to 2018. Capturing the Serie A and Coppa Italia title in the same year is often called the "domestic double." A double is a win of two major competitions in one season. A trebel is winning three. The Coppa Italia is Italy's national championship featuring 78 teams from the country's four professional leagues in a playoff-style format. Serie A teams are automatically let in to the round of 16, which happens before the quarterfinals.

THE LEGEND OF GIGI

One of the most beloved players on the Juventus teams of the 2000s was goalkeeper Gianluigi "Gigi" Buffon. Buffon spent the first six years of his Serie A career with another Italian team, Parma. He moved to Juventus in July 2001 for what was then a record amount of 59 million US dollars. Buffon's excellent goaltending led Juventus to nine Serie A titles. This was the most by any player in league history as of 2020. He spent 17 years with the club and played 656 games in all competitions.

Buffon had a Serie A "clean sheets" record until March 20, 2016. "Clean sheet" is a soccer term that also refers to a shutout, or when a goalie doesn't allow the other team to score a goal in a game. The game that day, against Torino, ended 4–1. Torino scored its only goal in the game's 48th minute. This also ended Buffon's record-setting mark of 974 consecutive minutes without allowing a goal.

Buffon set the single-season clean sheets record of 21 games in 2011–2012 and did it again in 2015–2016. During the 2015–2016 season, he shut out the opposition in 10 games in a row.

However, it was Buffon's actions following the 2005 Calciopoli scandal that Juventus fans will perhaps remember the most. The club was penalized, or punished, and sent to Serie B for one year. Several star players left the team to stay at Serie A with other clubs. Buffon stayed with Juventus to help the team return to Italy's top league. He then led Juventus to a 28-win Serie B championship season in 2006–2007. This meant that Juventus was back in Serie A the next season.

THE JUVENTUS WOMEN'S PROGRAM

Eniola Aluko of Juventus Women is shown here in her black and white jersey in 2018.

Juventus has had a successful youth program for many decades. There are programs for young men and young women. However, Juventus didn't have a professional adult women's team until 2017. That's when they bought the Serie A license of a team from Cuneo, Italy. This gave them the right to start a Juventus team with all new players.

Known as Juventus Women, the team entered the Serie A Femminile, or top women's league in Italy, for the 2017–2018 season. The team won 20 games in its first season and finished in a first-place tie with Italian women's team Brescia. Because of the tie, the two teams had to play each other in another game. Eventually, the game went to penalty kicks. Juventus defeated Brescia 5–4 to win the league title.

The team won a second Serie A title in 2018–2019 and has become very popular with Juventus soccer fans. In March 2019, the team played a game at Juventus Stadium in front of 39,000 fans. This broke the attendance record for an Italian women's league game at the time.

Buffon won the Serie A Goalkeeper of the Year award in 11 of his 17 seasons with Juventus. He was also selected as the Best European Goalkeeper three times.

GOLDEN YEARS

The Ballon d'Or (Golden Ball) is an award given each year to the player thought to be the world's best soccer player. Since it was first presented in 1956, a Juventus player has won several times. Michel Platini was the first player to win the Ballon d'Or for three straight years, from 1983 to 1985. Other Juventus winners include Pavel Nedved (2003), Zinedine Zidane (1998), Roberto Baggio (1993), Paolo Rossi (1982), and Omar Sivori (1961). In 2019, Cristiano Ronaldo and Matthijs de Ligt made the shortlist for the trophy.

Successes have been plentiful and help the team stay together and meet challenges. Winning and awards also happen because of the team's hard work and determination.

Gianluigi Buffon stops a penalty kick in UEFA Champions League action in 2016. He won 9 Serie A titles with Juventus over 17 seasons.

Michel Platini (*right*) chases down a ball against Kenny Dalglish (*left*) of Liverpool during the 1985 European Cup final at Heysel Stadium in Belgium.

4

MOVING FORWARD

To many, the world of professional sports seems like fun and games. What most people don't see are the challenges and important decisions that need to be made by people running the club. These decisions not only affect a team financially, but also how they are viewed by their fans. Over its history—and in the 21st century—Juventus has had difficulties and challenges too.

A STADIUM FOR ALL

Building a new stadium is a very important decision in sports. A stadium is a team's home. Teams try to create a unique experience for their players and fans inside the stadium. When a new stadium is built, it's a building where an entire community comes to life. Fans are a team's family. Teams want stadiums to be places fans enjoy visiting, giving them experiences they will never forget. The decision on how to build a new stadium and what it will look like is one that takes time and lots of money.

SPORT SHORT

Former Juventus captain Roberto Baggio was known as "Il Divin Codino" (The Divine Ponytail) during his career. That's because he liked to wear his hair in a long ponytail!

Sometimes, the decision to create a new stadium comes from past events that have changed a club forever. Juventus experienced a big event that changed them in 1985.

DISASTER

The 1985 European Cup final between Juventus and Liverpool was supposed to be a game between two of Europe's best teams. Instead, it became known as one of the saddest days in soccer history. Heysel Stadium in Brussels, Belgium, was the site of this big game. It was an old stadium—55 years old. Some people worried it was too old and run-down to handle a game this important. Officials from both teams wanted UEFA to move the game to another stadium. However, the decision was made to stay at Heysel.

A crowd of 58,000 people attended the game. The two end zones had standing room–only areas. Juventus fans were in one end zone area, and Liverpool supporters were in the other. The Liverpool end was divided into three separate sections labeled X, Y, and Z. Section Z was for locals or neutral fans. A neutral fan meant someone who wasn't cheering for either team; they just wanted to enjoy the game. Many Juventus fans made the trip to Brussels, and many ended up in section Z because it wasn't full.

With the Juventus fans now being so close to the Liverpool fan section, it created an uncomfortable situation before the game. There was only a thin fence separating the groups. The two groups were yelling at each other. Liverpool fans even began throwing rocks at the Juventus supporters. It wasn't long before they were able to knock down the fence. This meant the groups of angry fans from both teams now could come together and fight.

Afraid, some Juventus fans panicked and tried to leave the stadium. Soon, other fans were leaving too, but they were trapped by a large wall that was already falling apart. That wall eventually collapsed on them, killing 39 people (including 32 Italians) and injuring more than 500 others.

Despite the accident, the game was still played after a 90-minute delay. Juventus won 1–0 on a penalty kick from Michel Platini.

Police and fans are shown here helping victims caught in the disaster at Heysel Stadium in Belgium in 1985.

MONEYWISE

In their annual rankings of professional sports teams in June 2018, business magazine Forbes *figured out that Juventus was worth 1.47 billion US dollars. This made them the ninth most-valuable soccer team in the world.*

A team's overall value is based on a number of things, including how much money they make from selling tickets and team clothing like hats and jerseys. In 2018, the NFL's Dallas Cowboys were first overall with a value of $4.8 billion. They were followed by three European soccer teams in spots two through four: Manchester United ($4.123 billion), Real Madrid ($4.088 billion), and Barcelona ($4.064 billion). Juventus's total of $1.47 billion made them the most valuable soccer club in Italy at the time.

In a 2005 interview with UK newspaper the *Guardian*, Juventus player Paolo Rossi explained what it was like to play in that game:

> *The players were not aware of the true dimensions of the disaster. Some people said there was only one person dead and,*

really, we did not have any comprehensive information. It was only after the game that we were told the awful truth. We had been forced to play. We had no choice.

A long investigation found that Liverpool fans started the fighting. The team got a six-year ban from European competition. Several of the fans involved were also charged by police for their role in the incident.

CORRECTING PAST MISTAKES

Horrible incidents like the one at Heysel Stadium are those that teams never want to have happen again. Teams and soccer officials at all levels now meet regularly to talk about things that could possibly happen at games around the world and what they can do to make sure those things don't happen.

A report from UEFA.com in 2018 explained what teams need to be aware of at their stadiums for every game day now:

> *Regrettably, football [soccer] is no stranger to tragedy. Overcrowding, fires, pyrotechnics, violence and, more recently, terrorist threats, have been an unfortunate reality during the game's history, with lives lost or damaged on various occasions.*

Teams now have to keep these situations in mind when not only building new stadiums but also managing their current stadiums. This is something that Juventus had to remember when building their new stadium.

Because of the Heysel tragedy and a few similar events at other stadiums, no forms of fencing are allowed in stadiums today. Many stadiums also have to have seating for everyone. Juventus followed these rules at their stadium. There are no standing-room areas in the arena.

Juventus and many other teams across Europe also started using supporter cards around 2009. Just like a driver's license, a supporter card lists a fan's name, the city they live in, and what team they cheer for. These are required by teams when buying tickets to help prevent mixing fans from different teams in the same seating areas.

HOME SWEET HOME

When it came time to build a new stadium, Juventus management knew they had to do something special. They wanted Juventus Stadium to be about more than just the games. The stadium needed to be a place for Juventus fans from all the world, as well as a stadium for the locals to call their own.

One of the most important parts of the new stadium was to bring fans closer to the action on the field. The Stadio delle Alpi was the team's home from 1990 to 2006. One of the biggest complaints from fans was the massive size of the stadium. It held more than 70,000 fans and had a running track surrounding the field. This meant that fans were further away from the field than at most stadiums. When planning the new place, not only did the architects lower the number of seats in the new stadium, but they also made sure not to include a track in the design.

The state-of-the-art Juventus Stadium opened in 2011 and seats more than 41,000 fans.

Juventus Stadium was officially opened on September 8, 2011. It was built just north of Turin on the site of the Stadio delle Alpi that had been torn down in 2009. It took on a new name, Allianz Stadium, in July 2017 because of a sponsorship deal signed with Allianz, a German financial services company. Allianz paid Juventus $84 million to have its company name on the stadium until June 2023. Juventus hosted Notts County in the first game at Juventus Stadium. Notts County was the English team that gave Juventus its now classic black-and-white jerseys.

The 41,000-seat stadium cost an estimated $170 million to build and is the ultimate destination for Juventus fans. With 25,000 fewer seats than their previous stadium, Juventus fans are now closer to the action in a modern stadium setting that looks similar to many of the traditional English stadiums.

The stadium also produces much of its energy through solar panels. Concrete from the Stadio delle Alpi demolition was reused throughout the new building too.

A LIFETIME OF MEMORIES

Other than the games, the highlight for many visitors to the stadium is the Juventus Museum that opened in May 2012. Visitors to the museum can see the numerous trophies and souvenirs that highlight the club's memorable history. There's also a room that uses virtual reality technology to give fans a very special Juventus experience.

Architect Benedetto Camerana was the man responsible for designing the museum. He also designed the museums for Italian automobile companies Alfa Romeo and Ferrari. During its first six years of existence, the Juventus Museum hosted nearly 1.2 million visitors.

PERKS OF THE PITCH

One of the most unique features of the stadium area is J-Medical. This is a building located at the east end of Juventus Stadium. Opened in March 2016, this state-of-the-art medical facility operates in partnership with one of Italy's leading health-care companies. The medical building is open to everyone and is regularly used by Juventus players for injury treatment and helping them return from serious injuries.

THE REAL MADRID RIVALRY

Toni Kroos of Real Madrid (*left*) and Giorgio Chiellini of Juventus (*right*) battle during the 2017 UEFA Champions League Final.

Games between Juventus and Spanish team Real Madrid have become some of the most memorable in soccer history. Since they don't play in the same league, games between these two top teams always have more meaning when they play each other in European tournaments.

Based in Madrid, Spain, Real Madrid is one of the richest and most powerful soccer teams. Real Madrid plays in La Liga, the top professional league in Spain. They've won over 30 league titles since 1931, along with more than 12 UEFA Champions League titles.

All of the games between these teams have taken place in European Cup competition. They've met twice in the UEFA Cup final as of early 2020, and Real Madrid won both games. Real Madrid beat Juventus 1–0 in 1998, and again by a 4–1 score in 2017.

Juventus made the rivalry more interesting when the team signed superstar Cristiano Ronaldo away from Real Madrid in 2018.

The presence of J-Medical directly on the Juventus property is a huge advantage for the club. Most professional teams have some kind of medical facilities on site, but they often have to use local hospitals or doctors too. Juventus now has immediate access to world-class doctors and medical care just steps away from where they play and practice.

ROCKED BY SCANDAL

Relegation is also a challenge Juventus has had to overcome in the recent past. Juventus was sent down to Serie B for the 2006–2007 season after the Calciopoli scandal when police used telephone conversations to discover a link between team officials and referee organizations.

The police were trying to find out if the teams and referees were working together in an attempt to "fix" the results of games by selecting certain referees for particular games. "Fixing" a game is an illegal way to help create a specific final result in that game so that people who bet money can win more. Of the five teams involved, Juventus received the worst punishment. They were the only team relegated to Serie B.

Despite finishing first overall in Serie A in 2005–2006 with 27 wins, Juventus was assigned to last place and automatically relegated to Serie B for the 2006–2007 season. Internazionale finished second in the league and received the title instead. Juventus also had its 2004–2005 Serie A title removed. With the second-place team, AC Milan, also involved in the scandal, no league champion was awarded for the 2004–2005 Serie A season.

The scandal also resulted in several of Juventus's top players leaving the team. They didn't want to spend the 2006–2007 season playing in the lower-level Serie B. The biggest names to leave were Zlatan Ibrahimovic and Patrick Vieira, who went to Internazionale.

A group of players, including star goalkeeper Gianluigi Buffon and leading scorers Alessandro Del Piero and David Trezeguet, remained with Juventus, though. The team would need to finish as one of the top three teams of Serie B that season in order to qualify for promotion the next year.

Juventus excelled in Serie B with 28 wins and 4 losses. They won the league title and earned a promotion back to Serie A for the 2007–2008 season. This would be the one and only year in Juventus's history spent at the Serie B level as of 2020.

The Calciopoli scandal also uncovered many things that were being done wrong by the people running Italy's professional soccer leagues. A report about the scandal helped to start fixing the illegal things that were being done.

New evidence in the scandal has been revealed in recent years. It turns out that some teams may not have been as involved in the match fixing as the police first thought. This includes Juventus. Some European soccer officials are now saying the punishment handed out may have been an overreaction. Juventus has even gone to court to get their 2005–2006 Serie A championship back. Their most recent court appeal was made in September 2019.

Several Juventus players celebrate the team's eighth consecutive Serie A title on April 20, 2019.

5 LOOKING TO THE FUTURE

The Juventus teams that have won so many league championships in the 21st century are exactly the ones the Agnellis wanted to build back in 1923. It was their goal to become the best soccer team in Italy: strong, powerful, and dominant—not just for a few years, but for as many as possible. Today, the team is proving itself to be hungry for competition and for rewards for its hard work.

TODAY'S TEAM

Juventus made European soccer history by winning their eighth consecutive Serie A title in 2018–2019. It was the first time in any of Europe's five major leagues that a team had won eight straight league championships.

After winning the Serie A title in April 2019, former Juventus star and team vice president Pavel Nedved said, "I think a run like this will never be repeated again, especially in Italy, where it really is difficult to win titles. We won and won again with great players and coaches, but above all that particular Juventus mentality. The whole club deserves compliments, because it's crazy to win all these trophies."

In addition, championships are no longer just for male soccer players. On the same day that Juventus won their eighth straight Serie A title, April 20, 2019, the Juventus Women claimed their second consecutive Serie A title since they joined the league in 2017.

WHO'S NEXT?

The key to continuing success on the field is to have reliable players. Some of these players are showing their skills now. Juventus has its own youth training program called the Juventus Academy. The purpose of the program is to teach players who would like to play for I Bianconera in the future. The Juventus Academy consists of 17 boys' teams and is based in Vinovo, just outside of Turin.

The goal of the academy is to teach kids "the Juventus Way." This is a five-part process that tries to "develop footballers [soccer players] through a vision which combines technical aspects with mental, emotional and interpersonal ones." The academy isn't just about learning soccer skills. Players are taught to play the same way the professionals are.

Boys can join the academy as young as five years old. Former Juventus star Claudio Marchisio is one

SPORT SHORT

Juventus had over 65 million social media followers in 2019, with over 20 million on Instagram alone.

The members of Juventus under-19 pose for a team photo at the Juventus training center in 2019.

example of a player who learned the game at the Juventus Academy. Marchisio joined the academy at age seven on the "Primi Calci" (First Kicks) team. He went on to play 294 games over 11 seasons with Juventus from 2006 to 2018.

The academy's highest-level team is called the Primavera. This is the top team for young men between the ages of 15 and 20 who want to play professional soccer. Alessandro Del Piero and Roberto Bettega are the most famous Juventus players who played for the Primavera. Juventus also has training programs throughout the world in countries like the United States, Canada, and Mexico.

Born in February 2000, Moise Kean is another promising youth for the future of Juventus. He's a young player that will not only lead Juventus into the future, but also has the chance to become a star for the Italian national team. Part of the youth program, Kean has a natural ability to score goals. In May 2017, he became the first player born in the 2000s to score a goal in any of Europe's five professional soccer leagues. Kean was born in Italy, but his parents are from the Ivory Coast. This is a country on the south coast of West Africa.

THE RONALDO EFFECT

Juventus made headlines worldwide in July 2018 when they signed superstar Cristiano Ronaldo from Spain's Real Madrid. Ronaldo is considered by many to be the best soccer player in the world. He's a five-time winner of the Ballon d'Or award as of late 2019, and his transfer fee of $117 million was one of the highest ever paid.

Ronaldo had spent nine seasons with Real Madrid. He was the team's all-time leading scorer, and he led Real Madrid to win two La Liga championships and four Champions League titles. Ronaldo also played six seasons in the English Premier League with Manchester United from 2003 to 2009.

Ronaldo's signing with Juventus was another big move by the Agnelli family. This showed they wanted to remain one of the best teams in Serie A. It was also a way to add a top player who could help them win a Champions League title for the first time since 1996.

Ronaldo's popularity around the world gives Juventus the chance to become even more recognizable. The signing of Ronaldo had an immediate impact on everything from jersey sales to social media. Before Ronaldo even played a game with his new team, the effects of his signing were shown. More than 520,000 Juventus jerseys with Ronaldo's name on them

The addition of superstar Cristiano Ronaldo in July 2018 has meant tremendous success for Juventus both on and off the field.

were sold within 24 hours of going on sale for the first time. How impressive was this total? Juventus sold just 850,000 jerseys during the entire 2016–2017 season! Shortly after they signed Ronaldo, the team's various social media sites gained more than 1.5 million total followers in a single day.

FINDING A PLACE IN AMERICA

A 2016 report by an Italian research agency said that Juventus had 34 percent of the country's supporters, or *tifosi* in Italian. The team is now trying to become more popular in the United States. They've been growing in a few ways since. There are Juventus fan clubs throughout the world, including nine in the United States. Juventus has also played several noncompetition games (or friendlies) in the United States. In 2018, they played the Major League Soccer All-Stars before a crowd of 72,317 at Mercedes-Benz Stadium in Atlanta.

Juventus partnered with the NBA's Brooklyn Nets in 2018 to hold a Juventus Night at the Barclays Center during a Nets home game. Former Juventus star David Trezeguet was at the game along with Jay, the team mascot. After the event, Juventus gained 48,000 new American followers on Instagram and Facebook.

However, in summer 2019, the team decided not to visit the United States as part of their worldwide tour to see fans and play friendlies in the preseason.

Continuing to be a successful team isn't easy. Juventus is always keeping an eye on the future to stay at the top of its game worldwide. Whether it's adding a European player, developing the next big star at their academy, or building the best stadium possible, Juventus knows they must stay one step ahead of their competition to remain Italy's top team.

CHRONOLOGY

1897 The Sport-Club Juventus is officially formed by a group of high-school students in Turin, Italy.

1900 Juventus plays its first game in the Italian professional league.

1903 The team is renamed the Juventus Football Club.

1905 Juventus FC captures its first Italian League championship.

1923 The Agnelli family becomes the owner of Juventus.

1929 Juventus plays its first season in Serie A, Italy's top league.

1931 Juventus wins the first of five consecutive Serie A championships.

1938 Juventus wins their first Coppa Italia title.

1985 Juventus defeats Liverpool 1–0 to win its first European Cup championship.

1996 Juventus defeats Ajax on penalty kicks to claim their first Champions League title.

2006 The Calciopoli scandal relegates Juventus to Serie B for one season.

2011 Juventus Stadium officially opens on September 8.

2012 Juventus wins the Serie A title with an unbeaten record of 23 wins and 15 ties.

2015 Juventus sets the Italian league record with their 10th Coppa Italia title.

2017 The Juventus women's team launches.

2018 Cristiano Ronaldo transfers to Juventus from Real Madrid on July 10.

2019 Juventus's men's team wins their eighth consecutive Serie A title; the women's team wins the Serie A title too.

GLOSSARY

Ballon d'Or The award presented each year to the soccer player deemed to be the best in the world.

championship The final outcome of a season or series in sports to determine a winner.

clean sheet An achievement in soccer in which a team doesn't allow the opposition to score a goal against them in a game.

consecutive Describing an event happening right after another; in a row.

Coppa Italia The annual tournament that features the top teams from all four levels of Italian soccer.

derby One of the regular games played between two rivals based close to each other, usually in the same city or area.

dynasty A group or family that has been around for a long time.

FIFA The Fédération Internationale de Football Association, soccer's governing body.

forward A player who scores goals for a team and is primarily an offensive player. Also called a striker.

friendly A game between two teams that doesn't count in their league standings.

league A group of soccer teams that play each other in competitions.

manager Also referred to as the head coach; the person in charge of a team.

match An organized sporting event, also commonly referred to as a game.

pitch The playing field on which a soccer game takes place.

promotion The act of a team being moved up to a higher division because of their winning record.

relegation The process of moving a team down to a lower division because of their losing record.

scudetto Italian for "little shield," this is the jersey badge worn by the reigning Serie A champs.

Serie A The highest league in Italian professional soccer.

shutout An achievement in sports that occurs when a team doesn't allow the other team to score a goal.

tifosi An Italian term used to describe a group of passionate fans of one team or sport.

transfer The movement of a player from one team to another team for a set amount of money.

working class The group of people in a society who work for typically low wages in manufacturing or industrial work.

World Cup An international tournament between national teams that takes place every four years.

FURTHER INFORMATION

BOOKS

Digby, Adam. *Juventus: A History in Black & White.* Huddersfield, UK: Ockley Books, 2015.

DK. *The Soccer Book.* New York, NY: DK Publishing, 2018.

Gifford, Clive. *The Ultimate Champions League Fan Guide.* London, UK: Carlton Kids, 2015.

La Villa, Marco and Mauro. *The Juventus Story: Black & White Stripes.* New York, NY: Rizzoli, 2016.

Mandis, Steven G. *What Happened to Serie A: The Rise, Fall and Signs of Revival.* Edinburgh, UK: Arena Sport, 2018.

WEBSITES

ESPN.com: Serie A

www.espn.com/soccer/league/_/name/ita.1

ESPN's Serie A website keeps fans up to date with Serie A action and news.

Forza Italian Football Coverage

forzaitalianfootball.com

This website showcases all the action going on in soccer in Italy.

Official FIFA

www.fifa.com

The FIFA website explores the top governing body for soccer in the world.

Official Juventus

www.juventus.com/en

This is the official webpage for Juventus FC in English. You can find details about games, players, and team news.

VIDEOS

Black & White Stripes: The Juventus Story

This DVD discusses Juventus's history, told through the eyes of players, coaches, and others.

First Team: Juventus

This Netflix documentary explores the team throughout its history to today.

Official Juventus YouTube Channel

www.youtube.com/user/juventus

Visit this YouTube channel for game highlights and team memories.

SELECTED BIBLIOGRAPHY

Anderson, Cammy. "Juventus Lodge Another Appeal Against Calciopoli Scandal Decision To Award Inter 2006 Serie A Title." SempreInter.com. September 30, 2019. sempreinter.com/2019/09/30/juventus-lodge-another-appeal-against-calciopoli-scandal-decision-to-award-inter-2006-serie-a-title.

Chalmers, Robert. "Remembering the Heysel Stadium Disaster." GQ.com (UK). May 29, 2015. www.gq-magazine.co.uk/article/heysel-stadium-disaster-30-anniversary.

Gladwell, Ben. "Juventus Won't Add 3rd Star to Badge." ESPN.com. May 6, 2014. www.espn.com/soccer/news/story/_/id/1811729/juventus-add-star-badge-30th-title.

"Happy 90th Birthday, President Boniperti." Juventus.com. July 4, 2018. www.juventus.com/en/news/news/2018/90-birthday-boniperti-juventus.php.

"How Clubs Got Their Colours: Juventus." OutsideWrite.co.UK. outsidewrite.co.uk/clubs-got-colours-juventus.

Jackson, Jamie. "Heysel: The Witnesses' Stories." TheGuardian.com. April 3, 2005. www.theguardian.com/football/2005/apr/03/newsstory.sport.

"Juventus in New Calciopoli Appeal." Football-Italia.net. January 12, 2019. www.football-italia.net/133172/juventus-new-calciopoli-appeal.

Kidd, Robert. "Soccer Giants Juventus Eye U.S. Market To Attract Fans And Grow Brand." Forbes.com. January 13, 2019. www.forbes.com/sites/robertkidd/2019/01/13/soccer-giants-juventus-eye-us-market-to-attract-fans-and-grow-brand/#97f52fd1e419.

Lawrence, Amy. "Absent Friends Put Old Lady in Smaller Home." TheGuardian.com. March 19, 2006. www.theguardian.com/football/2006/mar/19/sport.comment1.

Ozanian, Mike. "The World's Most Valuable Soccer Teams." Forbes.com. June 12, 2018. www.forbes.com/sites/mikeozanian/2018/06/12/the-worlds-most-valuable-soccer-teams-2018/#5fe852fd45c8.

Ruiz, Marco. "Juventus Have 180 Million Fans World-Wide." AS.com. May 5, 2015. as.com/diarioas/2015/05/05/english/1430814781_116902.html.

Seal, Mark. "The Woman Who Wanted the Secrets." VanityFair.com. July 8, 2008. www.vanityfair.com/news/2008/08/agnelli200808.

"We Are #Le6end." Juventus.com. May 21, 2017. www.juventus.com/en/news/news/2017/juventus-champions-of-italy-for-the-sixth-time-in-a-row.php.

"When Juventus Played Their First Match." Medium.com. March 11, 2017. medium.com/whatahowler/when-juventus-played-their-first-match-b4318acc97fa.

INDEX

ABOUT THE AUTHOR

Kevin Snow is a Canadian-born sports and lifestyle freelance writer who has lived in Buffalo, New York, since 2000. Snow's professional career spans more than 25 years and includes 7 years in various editorial roles with *TV Guide Canada*, along with 10 seasons in public relations and marketing with the NHL's Buffalo Sabres. Snow has written for a variety of print and digital platforms in recent years, and has also been a contributor to the Associated Press, Canadian Press, and NHL.com. Snow credits his success to the support provided to him by his wife, Christine, and daughter, Alexandra.